CONTENTS

INTRODUCTION

What do you want your life to look like? Do you want to live with joy and peace no matter what comes your way? Do you want to wake up with a hopeful expectation for the future while also being grateful for the past?

This book offers you a path to make the abundant, overcoming life Jesus offers you a reality. We all have hopes and dreams, and we want to experience God's best and be a blessing to the people around us. Yet too often, setbacks, disappointments, and challenges chip away at our hope. Instead of thriving, we slip into survival mode and react to challenges with fear, offense, and doubt.

Thankfully, Jesus addressed this when He said: "*I have told you these things, so that in me you may have peace. In this world you will have trouble. But take heart! I have overcome the world*" (John 16:33).

Jesus knew we'd face struggles in this life, but He also assured us of victory. And in a vision God revealed to the prophet Ezekiel, we discover the key to experiencing the fulfillment of His promise.

In the story, Ezekiel finds himself in a valley of dry bones. Everywhere he looked, there was death and devastation. Then, God gave Ezekiel a surprising instruction. He said: "*Prophesy to these bones and say to them, 'Dry bones, hear the word of the* LORD'" (Ezekiel 37:4).

Ezekiel stood amidst darkness. But instead of giving voice to despair, he spoke God's Word. And something incredible happened!

> *So I prophesied as he commanded me,*
> *and breath entered them; they came to life*
> *and stood up on their feet—a vast army.*
> Ezekiel 37:10

Life followed his words! I share that story with you because there may be areas in your life that feel like they're filled with dry bones. If so, God is saying to you what He said to Ezekiel: *Speak words of faith and watch Me bring life to what looks dead!*

- Is your child struggling? It's time to start declaring, "My child will follow Jesus and fulfill their destiny."

- Are you battling an addiction? Declare, "I am free. Chains are breaking. This is not who God says I am."

- Are your finances under pressure? Declare, "I will lend and not borrow. Blessings are chasing me down!"

When our daughter, Alexandra, was four, she heard my wife, Victoria, and me talking about a friend who was dealing with headaches. Alexandra spoke up and said, “Daddy, I don’t have headaches, and I never will have headaches.” I thought, *You are prophesying the right thing!*

Soon after that, I was working on our garage door. It was stuck, and I was getting frustrated. I said under my breath, “This thing is never going to work.” Then I heard this little voice next to me say, “Daddy, you’re going to have what you say.”

It’s a lighthearted story, but my daughter was right. James 3:4 tells us that, like a small rudder steers a massive ship, the tongue sets the direction of our lives. Proverbs 18:21 goes even further. It says that the power of life and death are in the tongue and that we will eat the fruit of our words.

Think of words like seeds. If you want apples, you have to plant apple seeds. If you want oranges, you plant orange seeds. The harvest you hope for requires it. In the same way, your words need to align with God’s Word if you want to see His purpose and blessings come to pass in your life.

Make no mistake: the words you speak — about yourself and your future — will determine your reality. That's why in the pages ahead, you'll find powerful stories from Scripture and practical ways to align your words with God's promises so you can step into His best for you.

Negative words may have ensnared you in the past but today is a new day. In Jesus' name, I declare that strongholds are breaking in your life, hope is rising, and God is repositioning you for blessings, breakthrough, and victory!

THE WORDS YOU SPEAK ABOUT YOURSELF AND YOUR FUTURE WILL DETERMINE YOUR REALITY.

1

YOUR WORDS = VICTORY OR DEFEAT

"All those gathered here will know that it is not by sword or spear that the LORD saves; for the battle is the LORD's."

1 SAMUEL 17:47

The valley was tense. The Philistine army stood on one side. The Israelites on the other. For forty days, the Philistines had sent out their champion to taunt Israel's army. His name was Goliath, a giant who stood nearly ten feet tall. The armor he wore weighed 125 pounds. Yet, it wasn't his size and strength alone that were intimidating. It was his words.

> *"Why do you come out and line up for battle? Am I not a Philistine, and are you not the servants of Saul? Choose a man and have him come down to me. If he is able to fight and kill me, we will become your subjects; but if I overcome him and kill him, you will become our subjects and serve us" . . . "This day I defy the armies of Israel! Give me a man and let us fight each other."* 1 Samuel 17:8–10

Every morning and evening, the scene repeated itself. Goliath spoke and fear spread. Words were winning the battle long before a sword was lifted.

Then David arrived. He wasn't a soldier. He wasn't trained for war. He was a young boy, a shepherd, delivering food to his brothers in Israel's army. But when David heard Goliath's words, something stirred within him. While everyone else saw impossibility, David heard an insult against God.

> *"Who is this uncircumcised Philistine that he should defy the armies of the living God?"*
> 1 Samuel 17:26

When David went before King Saul to announce his intention to fight Goliath, Saul tried to talk him out of it! But David would not be moved:

> *"When a lion or a bear came and carried off a sheep from the flock, I went after it, struck it and rescued the sheep from its mouth. When it turned on me, I seized it by its hair, struck it and killed it. . . . This uncircumcised Philistine will be like one of them, because he has defied the armies of the living God. The* LORD *who rescued me from the paw of the lion and the paw of the bear will rescue me from the hand of this Philistine."*
> 1 Samuel 17:34–37

King Saul tried to outfit David with his very own sword and armor. But David, in essence, told him, "Thank you, but no." He didn't need weapons of bronze; He only needed his staff and five smooth stones for his slingshot.

Finally, David stood face-to-face with Goliath on the battlefield. The giant mocked him, *"Am I a dog, that you come at me with sticks?"* (v. 43). It was at that moment David had to make the choice again: agree with the voice of defeat or declare victory. He replied, *"You come against me with sword and spear and javelin, but I come against you in the name of the* LORD *Almighty. . . . This day the* LORD *will deliver you into my hands"* (vv. 45–46).

David didn't say, "I hope." He didn't say, "Maybe." He said, *"This day."* The battle was settled in his words before it was settled in the valley.

> *As the Philistine moved closer to attack him, David ran quickly toward the battle line to meet him. Reaching into his bag and taking out a stone, he slung it and struck the Philistine on the forehead. The stone sank into his forehead, and he fell facedown on the ground. So David triumphed over the Philistine with a sling and a stone; without a sword in his hand he struck down the Philistine and killed him.* 1 Samuel 17:48–50

DAVID'S VICTORY WASN'T ABOUT SIZE, STRENGTH, OR STRATEGY. IT WAS ABOUT HIS WORDS RELEASING GOD'S POWER! IN THE SAME WAY, WHEN YOU SPEAK VICTORY, YOU'RE NOT DENYING REALITY. YOU ARE DECLARING THE TRUTH THAT GOD HAS THE FINAL WORD.

VICTORY

Every day, people and circumstances will try to tell you who you are, what you can't do, and how your story is going to turn out. Discouragement may come from all directions — a medical report, a bank statement, a past mistake, a painful disappointment, or a delay that's lasted far longer than you expected. The opposition or obstacle standing in your way can feel overwhelming, like a giant taunting you.

For David, it was a *literal* giant! But here's one of the most powerful details in the story: David never once referred to Goliath as a giant. He never said, "He's so big," or "Look how strong he is." And those statements would have been true. David saw the same massive warrior the rest of the Israelite army saw. He knew the same facts. He understood the same risks. Yet David refused to let the situation name him, define him, or intimidate him.

David called Goliath an *"uncircumcised Philistine."* You see, David wasn't ignoring the fact Goliath was big. He simply remembered God was bigger and that if Goliath dared speak against God and His people, his fate was already sealed.

David understood something:
You don't put your problem on the throne.
You keep God on the throne!

In moments of stress and difficulty, it's easy to magnify our problems and minimize God. We replay the bad report, rehearse the fear, and repeat the worst-case scenario. But the voice of victory does the opposite. It magnifies God and puts the problem in its proper place — at His feet!

It's no accident that David wrote in Psalm 103:19, *The Lord has established his throne in heaven, and his kingdom rules over all.*

Let me encourage you to follow David's example. Don't think about how big your problem is. Reflect on how big your God is. Debt can loom large, but God promises to provide (Psalm 37:25). Cancer has a name, but there is a *Name* that is higher than any other (Philippians 2:9). That obstacle may look intimidating, but it's only temporary. The question is, *what (or who) is on your throne today?*

- Instead of saying, "This is such a big challenge," say, "I serve a big God. Nothing is too difficult for Him."

- Instead of saying, "Another setback. I didn't get the promotion," say, "I know God has something better. He is working everything together for my good."

- Instead of saying, "I'll never meet the right person," say, "Something good will happen to me. Divine connections are coming my way."

- If someone says, "I heard you got a bad medical report," respond, "Yes, but I have another report. God is restoring health unto me."

- If someone says, "I heard they did you wrong," you can say, "Yes, but I'm not bitter. God is my Vindicator. He's giving me beauty for ashes."

Another important moment I want to highlight is when David spoke with King Saul. He said, "*The* L*ORD* *who rescued me from the paw of the lion and the paw of the bear will rescue me from the hand of this Philistine*" (1 Samuel 17:37).

Here's the principle: the victories you've already experienced are evidence that God is still working on your behalf. The same God who delivered you before is the same God who will bring you through again. And if your faith is weary and you feel like you haven't seen His victory in your life, receive this prayer written by David himself in Psalm 20.

> *May the LORD answer you when you are in distress; may the name of the God of Jacob protect you. May he send you help from the sanctuary and grant you support from Zion.May he remember all your sacrifices and accept your burnt offerings. May he give you the desire of your heart and make all your plans succeed.May we shout for joy over your victory and lift up our banners in the name of our God. May the LORD grant all your requests. Now this I know: The LORD gives victory to his anointed. He answers him from his heavenly sanctuary with the victorious power of his right hand. Some trust in chariots and some in horses, but we trust in the name of the LORD our God.*
> Psalm 20:1-7 (NIV)

When David ran toward Goliath, he didn't say, "I hope this works." He didn't say, "Let's see what happens." He said, *"The battle is the LORD's"*

(1 Samuel 17:47). He declared victory before the giant ever fell.

When you speak victory, peace, healing, and hope — even when you don't see it yet — you are declaring that God has the final word, because He does!

> *But thanks be to God! He gives us the victory through our Lord Jesus Christ.*
> 1 Corinthians 15:57

When the victory comes, you'll look back and realize it started the moment you opened your mouth and spoke what God's already said.

IF, RIGHT NOW, YOUR WORDS = DEFEAT . . .

"

~~*I can't ever seem to get this right.*~~

~~*I just don't see any hope in this situation.*~~

~~*Things just seem to keep going wrong in my life.*~~

"

CHANGE THEM!
LET YOUR WORDS =
VICTORY

"

I can do all things through Christ who strengthens me.

I have a hope that is firm and secure. Victory is coming!

God has a hope and a future for me. I will overcome through Christ who has already overcome for me!

"

SCRIPTURES FOR VICTORY

But thanks be to God! He gives us the victory through our Lord Jesus Christ.

1 CORINTHIANS 15:57

No, in all these things we are more than conquerors through him who loved us.

ROMANS 8:37

For everyone born of God overcomes the world. This is the victory that has overcome the world, even our faith.

1 JOHN 5:4

"For the LORD *your God is the one who goes with you to fight for you against your enemies to give you victory."*

DEUTERONOMY 20:4

But thanks be to God, who always leads us as captives in Christ's triumphal procession and uses us to spread the aroma of the knowledge of him everywhere.

2 CORINTHIANS 2:14

Through you we push back our enemies; through your name we trample our foes.

PSALM 44:5

The horse is made ready for the day of battle, but victory rests with the LORD.

PROVERBS 21:31

"The LORD *is my strength and my defense; he has become my salvation."*

EXODUS 15:2

"No weapon forged against you will prevail, and you will refute every tongue that accuses you."

ISAIAH 54:17

"Do not be afraid or discouraged because of this vast army. For the battle is not yours, but God's."

2 CHRONICLES 20:15

With God we will gain the victory, and he will trample down our enemies.

PSALM 60:12

"In this world you will have trouble. But take heart! I have overcome the world."

JOHN 16:33

The God of peace will soon crush Satan under your feet.

ROMANS 16:20

2

YOUR WORDS = BLESSING OR BURNOUT

"Because you say so, I will let down the nets."

LUKE 5:5

The sun was beginning to rise over the Sea of Galilee as Simon Peter and the fishermen with him pulled their boats to the shore.

It had been a long night marked by effort more than reward. Hour after hour, they cast their nets and adjusted their strategy. Fishing wasn't a hobby for them; it was their livelihood. Yet, they were empty-handed.

No fish meant no income. No fish meant stress, disappointment, and the quiet frustration that settles in when you've done everything right and still have nothing to show for it. Peter's muscles probably ached. His hands may have been raw. His body was surely exhausted and his hope used up as well.

A crowd started to gather nearby. A new teacher was approaching. By this point, Peter had likely heard of Jesus, the man who spoke with authority and healed the sick.

Jesus asked Peter if He could use his boat to address the crowd. Peter agreed and pushed the boat out just enough for Jesus to speak. Peter surely listened as He taught, hearing words that were powerful and filled with truth and compassion. Still, Peter's mind may have drifted back to the empty nets.

When Jesus finished, He turned to Peter and said something unexpected: *"Put out into deep water, and let down the nets for a catch"* (Luke 5:4).

Everything in Peter had a reason to object. Jesus wasn't a fisherman. It was the wrong time of day. The fish wouldn't be there. And beyond that, he was still tired! He answered honestly, *"Master, we've worked hard all night and haven't caught anything"* (v. 5).

You can feel the weariness in his words. Peter didn't stop there, however. He added, *"But because you say so, I will let down the nets"* (v. 5).

Those words weren't spoken from a place of overflowing faith. I doubt Peter felt energized or suddenly confident. Nevertheless, he chose to align his words with Jesus anyway.

Peter pushed back out into the water. He lowered the net again — despite his experience, instincts, and fatigue telling him it wouldn't work. Then, a tug. Then, another. The net grew heavy. Too heavy. Fish filled it, more than Peter had ever seen in one catch!

He shouted to another boat for help. Water splashed. The two boats rocked, nearly sinking with the weight of the catch. Moments earlier, Peter was burned out. Now, he stood in the middle of an overflowing blessing!

Astonished and ashamed, Peter fell at Jesus' feet. *"Go away from me, Lord; I am a sinful man!"* (v. 8). The miracle didn't inflate his ego; it humbled him. He understood that this blessing wasn't about fish. It was about Jesus. It was about a God who could bring blessing where there had only been burnout.

Jesus looked at him and said, *"Don't be afraid; from now on you will fish for people"* (v. 10).

Peter's words had moved him from burnout to blessing and then from blessing into purpose. What he thought was a useless night on the sea became the day his destiny came into focus.

Peter and those with him pulled their boats up to shore, left everything, and followed Jesus.

YOU MIGHT BE IN A SEASON WHERE YOUR NET FEELS EMPTY. YOU'VE BEEN FAITHFUL. YOU'VE WORKED HARD. YOU'VE PRAYED AND HOPED, AND NOW YOU'RE TIRED. BUT WHAT IF YOUR NEXT STEP OF OBEDIENCE TO GOD IS THE ONE THAT RELEASES BLESSING AND PURPOSE?

Peter's story began in a place many of us know all too well: burnout.

Burnout can happen when you're doing the right thing but nothing seems to work right. You're showing up to work each day, trying your best in college, praying for that loved one to return to the Lord, and yet, the efforts feel like they're in vain. You're weary, not just physically but emotionally and spiritually.

That's how Peter felt when Jesus stepped into his boat. And when Jesus told him to try again, Peter answered with a remarkably human response: "*Master, we've worked hard all night*" (Luke 5:5).

Peter didn't deny his fatigue at that moment. But — and this is so important — he refused to let it have the final word. He chose obedience over discouragement. And obedience positioned him for overflow.

The situation didn't look promising for catching fish. The conditions hadn't changed. What *did* change, however, was his response to Jesus' word. He obeyed, not because it made sense but because

Jesus said so. And the moment he did, blessing rushed in.

In the same way, maybe you're going to work, raising your kids, and fulfilling your daily responsibilities — doing it all. It can feel like a night of trying to catch some fish yet returning to shore empty and burned out. In those moments, God is inviting you to step back out onto the sea again. Only, this time, not in your strength or strategy but in His.

Personally, this happened when I heard the Compaq Center was available to purchase. Lakewood Church needed a larger auditorium, but everything in my mind said, *There's no way. The city's not going to let a church have it. We don't know the right people. It's going to be too expensive.*

I thought of a hundred excuses for why it couldn't happen. Yet, in my spirit, I could hear a still, small voice saying, *That building is ours. God is making a way.* Even then, I didn't have the desire or faith to believe for it. I was weary and burned out. But do you know what happened? God made a way!

If you've ever bought a small electronic device like a flashlight or clock, you'll sometimes see a sticker on it that says, "Batteries included." The device on its own won't do you any good. You need batteries to power it.

When God gives you instruction, when you hear that still, small voice telling you to do something, you don't only get the instruction. Batteries are included, and that's the power of the Holy Spirit!

Has God asked you to do something that doesn't make sense? It may not be to purchase a former sports arena or go fishing at the wrong time of day, but could it be to forgive that person who did you wrong? Could it be to act generously toward someone in your life when you're barely getting by?

Psalm 36:5–9 proclaims this blessing:

> *Your unfailing love, O LORD, is as vast as the heavens; your faithfulness reaches beyond the clouds. Your righteousness is like the mighty mountains, your justice like the ocean depths. You care for people and animals alike, O LORD. How precious is your unfailing love, O God! All humanity finds shelter in the shadow of your*

wings. You feed them from the abundance of your own house, letting them drink from your river of delights. For you are the fountain of life, the light by which we see (NLT).

Remember, Jesus didn't rebuke Peter for being tired. He simply invited him to obey, and obedience turned burnout into blessing. And do you remember what happened after?

Peter fell at Jesus' feet, humbled and apologetic. But Jesus didn't condemn him. He declared a new calling over him: *"From now on you will fish for people"* (Luke 5:10).

I wonder what calling God will make clear to you in the days ahead as you obey His Word.

Peter could have gone home. Instead, he obeyed. And when blessing came, it wasn't small. It wasn't barely enough. It was more than he could manage on his own. And the same can be true for you!

IF, RIGHT NOW, YOUR WORDS = **BURNOUT . . .**

“

~~*I’m exhausted.*~~

~~*I’ve tried everything and don’t have anything left.*~~

~~*Nothing is working right.*~~

”

CHANGE THEM! LET YOUR WORDS = BLESSING

"

God is renewing my strength.

Because God says so, I won't give up. God's grace is sufficient for me.

God can bring blessing out of any situation.

"

SCRIPTURES FOR BLESSING

Commit to the LORD whatever you do,
and he will establish your plans.

PROVERBS 16:3

And God is able to bless you abundantly, so that in all things at all times, having all that you need, you will abound in every good work.

2 CORINTHIANS 9:8

"My grace is sufficient for you, for my power is made perfect in weakness."

2 CORINTHIANS 12:9

"Come to me, all you who are weary and burdened, and I will give you rest."

MATTHEW 11:28

But those who hope in the LORD will renew their strength. They will soar on wings like eagles; they will run and not grow weary, they will walk and not be faint.

ISAIAH 40:31

Trust in the LORD with all your heart and lean not on your own understanding; in all your ways submit to him, and he will make your paths straight.

PROVERBS 3:5–6

Let us not become weary in doing good, for at the proper time we will reap a harvest if we do not give up.

GALATIANS 6:9

You prepare a table before me in the presence of my enemies. . . . My cup overflows.

PSALM 23:5

All these blessings will come on you and accompany you if you obey the LORD your God.

DEUTERONOMY 28:2

"I am the vine; you are the branches. If you remain in me and I in you, you will bear much fruit; apart from me you can do nothing."

JOHN 15:5

We went through fire and water, but you brought us to a place of abundance.

PSALM 66:12

But whoever looks intently into the perfect law that gives freedom, and continues in it . . . they will be blessed in what they do.

JAMES 1:25

3

YOUR WORDS = AGREEMENT OR DISPUTE

"I am the Lord's servant," Mary answered.
"May your word to me be fulfilled."

LUKE 1:38

Mary was young when the angel Gabriel appeared to her. She was living a quiet life and preparing for marriage. Nothing hinted that Heaven itself was about to step into her world. Suddenly, it did: *"Greetings, you who are highly favored. The Lord is with you"* (Luke 1:28).

Scripture says Mary was troubled at the angel's greeting, and you can understand why. Favor didn't feel obvious. She wasn't royalty. She wasn't famous. She was just Mary. Yet, here stood a messenger from Heaven, declaring God had set His affection on her in an extraordinary way.

As Gabriel continued speaking, the words felt even more impossible. She would conceive and give birth to a son, a child promised long ago, a king whose reign would never end. And she would do this without ever knowing a man.

As she heard those words, she marveled: *"How will this be . . . ?"* (Luke 1:34). The angel didn't scold her for the question. He reassured her. The Holy Spirit would overshadow her. Then, almost tenderly, Gabriel pointed her to Elizabeth, her older cousin, who was miraculously six months pregnant. Then, he left her with a promise that still steadies hearts today: *"No word from God will ever fail"* (Luke 1:37).

Mary faced a choice. She could reason it all away. She could dismiss it as too risky, unbelievable, and costly. But instead, in one of the most beautiful responses in all of Scripture, she surrendered: *"I am the Lord's servant."* . . . *"May your word to me be fulfilled"* (Luke 1:38).

After the angel left, real life rushed back in. There were conversations to have and explanations to make. She had to look Joseph in the eyes and tell him something that sounded impossible, even to her own ears — that an angel had spoken and that she was carrying a child conceived by God.

Heartbroken and confused, Joseph decided to end their engagement, until Heaven interrupted him too. An angel visited him in a dream, and Joseph made his own powerful choice to trust God and stay.

Not long after, Mary made the journey to visit Elizabeth. When she arrived and called out her greeting, something extraordinary happened. At the sound of Mary's voice, Elizabeth's baby leapt inside her, as if the miracle within Mary awakened the miracle within Elizabeth.

Filled with the Holy Spirit, Elizabeth spoke a blessing over her young cousin, marveling that Mary believed what the Lord had said would come to pass.

Two women, both carrying promises that looked impossible, stood together rejoicing, strengthening one another's faith.

In time, Elizabeth gave birth to John the Baptist, the forerunner. And Mary gave birth to Jesus, the Savior of the world.

Yet, within these stories stands a contrast. Elizabeth's husband, Zechariah, also received the same angelic promise his wife did, but his first response was calculation — age, biology, and limitation. He measured the Word of God against what seemed reasonable. And for a season, he couldn't speak, as though Heaven guarded the atmosphere around the promise, keeping doubt from taking root.

All through these moments runs a timeless truth: when God speaks, agreement creates space for the miraculous.

Mary didn't understand everything. She still had questions and faced uncertainty. But she chose trust over logic and surrender over control. She stayed close to people of faith, kept her heart aligned with what God said, and, step by step, watched the impossible unfold!

AGREEMENT

WHEN ONE YOUNG WOMAN SAID YES TO GOD'S WORD, THE WORLD WAS NEVER THE SAME. THE QUESTION IS, HOW ARE YOU RESPONDING TO WHAT GOD IS SPEAKING TO YOU?

So often we think fulfilling God's Word and promises in our lives is about talent, resources, and perfect timing. Many times, however, it comes down to something much simpler and quieter — whether we choose to agree with God or argue with Him.

Mary didn't understand what the angel was asking of her. How could she? Nothing about it made logical sense. Yet, with questions swirling and the future unclear, she chose to agree with God. Not because she had proof. Not because it felt safe. But because she trusted the One who spoke.

Elizabeth did the same. After years of disappointment and prayers that seemed unanswered, she could have guarded her heart. She could have refused to hope for a child again. Instead, when God moved, she received the miracle with faith.

Neither woman had the whole picture. Neither could explain the process. But both aligned their words with God's Word. And miracles followed!

It's easy to read those stories and think they belong to another time or another world. But the principle hasn't changed. The same God still speaks promises, and He's looking for people who will come into agreement with what He says.

A promise from God won't force itself into your life. It looks for agreement. It looks for a heart that says, "Yes!"

There will be other voices that question, minimize, and plant doubt in your heart. Sometimes they'll come from people around you. Other times they'll come from your own thoughts late at night.

"That's too big," they'll say. "That's unrealistic," they'll whisper. "Don't get your hopes up," they'll sarcastically speak. And the moment you verbalize a thought, you give it permission to take root.

If Mary had listened to voices like that, history may have read differently. Instead, she simply said, "*Let it be to me*" (Luke 1:38, ESV).

That small sentence didn't make her path easier. It didn't remove the questions or the risks. But it aligned her heart with Heaven. When you come into agreement with God like that, something begins to shift behind the scenes. Doors you couldn't open start opening. The right people show up. Connections form. What God planted in you starts taking root.

Agreement doesn't mean you never wrestle with doubt or fear. It just means you trust God more and give Him room to carry you through. Mary declared, *"I am the Lord's servant"* (Luke 1:38). In other words, "God, my life is Yours. I may not understand the process, but I trust You."

Contrast that with Zechariah. He loved God. He served diligently as a priest. But when his promise came, he measured it against logic instead of faith. And for a season, his voice fell silent — not as punishment but as protection, as if God was shielding the promise from words that could undermine it.

It's a reminder that what we say carries weight. Our words can either agree with Heaven or argue against it.

I've learned in my own life that agreement also affects those who walk with you. When Mary received her promise, God didn't leave her isolated. He led her straight to Elizabeth, someone who understood, who would strengthen her faith instead of weakening it. And when those two women stood together, both carrying miracles, something beautiful happened.

Joy filled the room. Faith fed faith. Elizabeth's baby leapt! That's what agreement does. It draws the right people into your life — people who speak life when you feel unsure and who remind you of God's promise when you're tempted to forget.

Elizabeth declared over Mary, "*Blessed is she who has believed that the Lord would fulfill his promises to her!*" (Luke 1:45). That's the kind of friend we all need.

Finally, there's something else worth highlighting in Mary's story: agreement changes the atmosphere.

Yes, Mary still had explaining to do. Elizabeth still had months to wait. But the moment they agreed with God, the miracle was set in motion. And the same is true for you.

When you choose to agree with God and say, "This promise is for me. God is working. My best days are still ahead" — His Word moves from being theoretical to personal. It stops being something you admire from a distance and becomes something you live on a day-to-day basis.

Second Corinthians 1:20 says, *For no matter how many promises God has made, they are "Yes" in Christ. And so through him the "Amen" is spoken by us to the glory of God.*

That "*Amen*" is what Mary spoke: "*May your word to me be fulfilled*" (Luke 1:38). That "*Amen*" is what Elizabeth stood on. That "*Amen*" became the posture of Joseph's heart. That "*Amen*" is what Zechariah at first refused to reconcile with his circumstances.

What will be your response? Remember, responding to God's Word isn't about figuring everything out. It doesn't mean having all the answers. It isn't about seeing the future with perfect clarity. It's about a faith consisting of a quiet, steady "yes." Because, sometimes, that's all Heaven needs.

IF, RIGHT NOW, YOUR WORDS = DISPUTE . . .

"

~~*There's no way this can happen.*~~

~~*I need to figure this out myself.*~~

~~*God, I don't see how Your Word will be fulfilled.*~~

"

CHANGE THEM! LET YOUR WORDS = AGREEMENT

"*The Lord is my strength and salvation.*

God is opening doors for me I may not understand.

No matter what I see or don't understand, I will trust You!"

SCRIPTURES FOR AGREEMENT

"Again, truly I tell you that if two of you on earth agree about anything they ask for, it will be done for them by my Father in heaven."

MATTHEW 18:19

"Do two walk together unless they have agreed to do so?"

AMOS 3:3

"The tongue has the power of life and death, and those who love it will eat its fruit."

PROVERBS 18:21

"So is my word that goes out from my mouth: It will not return to me empty, but will accomplish what I desire and achieve the purpose for which I sent it."

ISAIAH 55:11

"Truly I tell you, if anyone says to this mountain, 'Go, throw yourself into the sea,' and does not doubt in their heart but believes that what they say will happen, it will be done for them."

MARK 11:23

But when you ask, you must believe and not doubt, because the one who doubts is like a wave of the sea, blown and tossed by the wind.

JAMES 1:6

Let us hold unswervingly to the hope we profess, for he who promised is faithful.

HEBREWS 10:23

For no matter how many promises God has made, they are "Yes" in Christ. And so through him the "Amen" is spoken by us to the glory of God.

2 CORINTHIANS 1:20

May the God who gives endurance and encouragement give you the same attitude of mind toward each other that Christ Jesus had, so that with one mind and one voice you may glorify the God and Father of our Lord Jesus Christ.

ROMANS 15:5–6

This day I call the heavens and the earth as witnesses against you that I have set before you life and death, blessings and curses. Now choose life, so that you andyour children may live.

DEUTERONOMY 30:19

"What you decide on will be done, and light will shine on your ways."

JOB 22:28

"If you believe, you will receive whatever you ask for in prayer."

MATTHEW 21:22

Then make my joy complete by being like-minded, having the same love, being one in spirit and of one mind.

PHILIPPIANS 2:2

This is the confidence we have in approaching God: that if we ask anything according to his will, he hears us. And if we know that he hears us—whatever we ask—we know that we have what we asked of him

1 JOHN 5:14–15

May these words of my mouth and this meditation of my heart be pleasing in your sight, LORD, my Rock and my Redeemer.

PSALM 19:14

4

YOUR WORDS = FAITH OR FEAR

Then Caleb silenced the people before Moses and said, "We should go up and take possession of the land, for we can certainly do it."

NUMBERS 13:30

Twelve men returned to the Israelite camp after exploring a land that was rich and overflowing with promise, exactly as God said it would be. For forty days they had walked its valleys, surveyed its cities, and tasted its fruit. Now, all of Israel waited to hear what they would say.

Moses stood at the front, surrounded by a nation that had seen the hand of God move again and again. They had watched the Nile turn to blood and saw darkness cover Egypt while their own homes were filled with light. They had been delivered from slavery and crossed the Red Sea on dry ground. They had followed a pillar of cloud by day and fire by night. This moment, at the threshold of the Promised Land, was what all of it had been leading toward.

At first, the report was encouraging. *"We went into the land to which you sent us,"* the spies said, *"and it does flow with milk and honey!"* (Numbers 13:27). They lifted the fruit as proof. But then things took a turn: *"But the people who live there are powerful, and the cities are fortified and very large. We even saw descendants of Anak there"* (v. 28).

They were giants! Fear crept into the air. The spies began to magnify the obstacles. *"We can't attack those people; they are stronger than we are"* (v. 31). Another voice added, *"We seemed like grasshoppers in our own eyes, and we looked the same to them"* (v. 33).

With those words, faith drained from the camp. Murmurs turned into complaints. Confidence dissolved into panic. Soon, the people began weeping aloud, saying, *"If only we had died in Egypt! . . . Why is the LORD bringing us to this land only to let us fall by the sword?"* (Numbers 14:2–4). Some even suggested choosing a new leader and going back to slavery.

But two men couldn't stay silent. Joshua and Caleb stepped forward and quieted the people. *"The land we passed through is exceedingly good. If the LORD is pleased with us, he will lead us into that land. And do not be afraid"* (vv. 7–9).

All twelve of the spies had seen the same land. They had walked the same terrain and faced the same realities. The difference wasn't in what they saw but in how they interpreted it.

Ten spies focused on the size of the giants. Two focused on the size of their God.

Nevertheless, the people believed the fearful report. And with that decision, what could have been an eleven-day journey to the Promised Land became forty years of wandering in the wilderness. Names like Sethur, Gaddiel, and Shaphat faded into history — not because they lacked opportunity but because they were three of the spies who chose fear over faith.

Joshua and Caleb were different. Years later, they were still standing.

When Moses's time came to an end, Joshua was chosen to lead. Again, the people stood at the edge of promise, this time facing the Jordan River at flood stage, their entry point to the land God promised them. But Joshua's words weren't filled with fear. *"Consecrate yourselves,"* he told the people, *"for tomorrow the* Lord *will do amazing things among you"* (Joshua 3:5). When the priests stepped into the water the next day, it stopped flowing!

Faith made a way where fear had stalled progress. You see, the Promised Land was never withheld because of giants. It was delayed because of perspective. The promise had never changed. The only thing that shifted was which words the people chose to believe and speak.

WHAT'S YOUR "PROMISED LAND"? WHAT DREAM HAS GOD PLACED IN YOUR HEART THAT FEELS JUST OUT OF REACH? WHAT HEALING ARE YOU BELIEVING FOR? WHAT NEW BEGINNING ARE YOU STANDING ON THE EDGE OF, EVEN NOW?

FAITH

Fear has a subtle way of making friends with what's familiar. Fear whispers, "Just stay here. Don't risk it. Don't believe too big. Don't expect too much. At least this is safe." But faith doesn't talk like that.

Faith takes the limits off what God can do in your future. Faith says, "There's more in you than you realize. God has already gone ahead of you. Step forward. Trust Him. The promise is bigger than the problem!"

That quiet tension between fear and faith has followed God's people from the very beginning, and you can see it so clearly in the story of the twelve spies Moses sent into the Promised Land.

All twelve men walked across the same ground. They felt the same sun on their backs. They saw the same cluster of grapes so large they had to be hung on poles between two of them. They saw the same fortified cities rising in the distance and the same giants moving through the land.

The facts weren't different. The landscape wasn't different. Their *perspective* was.

Ten of them came back rehearsing everything that could go wrong. You can almost hear the strain in their voices as they described the obstacles — the thick walls, the size of the armies, how small and incapable they felt by comparison. They didn't just bring information; they brought fear. "We can't do this," they said. "We don't have a chance. We look like grasshoppers next to them."

What they didn't realize was that they weren't just describing the situation. They were prophesying their future. Their words didn't simply express fear; their words framed their destiny. Day after day, they agreed with defeat, and eventually defeat became their reality. They never stepped into the land God promised, not because God failed them but because fear convinced them to settle for less.

Joshua and Caleb, however, stood on the same soil and saw the same giants. Yet, something sounded different in their voices. They didn't deny the challenges. They didn't pretend the opposition wasn't real.

"Yes, the cities are strong," they said. "Yes, the people are big. But our God is greater. We are well able. Let us go in at once."

They weren't about to let any form of opposition stifle their faith for what God promised. The question is, *What's your promised land?*

Fear will try to talk you out of it. Fear will tell you you're too late, too inexperienced, too ordinary. Fear will try to send you backward to what's familiar — even if familiar means settling for a life that's smaller than what God intended.

Faith calls you *forward*.

I think about a moment in my own life that reminds me how faithful God is. Years ago, I was driving on the freeway in heavy rain when my car suddenly hit the guardrail and started spinning across five lanes of traffic. Everything slowed down. I remember facing the wrong direction and seeing an eighteen-wheeler coming straight toward me. For a split second, it felt like time stood still. I thought, *This is it.*

I didn't have time for a long prayer or perfect words. All I could say was one name: "Jesus." The next thing I knew, my car had come to rest safely on the shoulder. The truck driver told me a sudden gust of wind pushed him into the next lane at the last second. He called it luck. I knew better. It was the hand of God.

We all have moments like that — moments we can look back at and say, "By this, I know the Lord is on my side."

Those memories aren't just stories to revisit; they're fuel for your faith. When new challenges show up and giants appear, you can remember what God has already done. Something inside you can rise up and say, *If He did it before, He'll do it again.*

Joshua and Caleb did this. They recalled the miracles in Egypt, the parting of the Red Sea, and the miraculous provision of food in the wilderness.

Centuries later, the apostle Paul echoed this truth when he said, *"I live by faith in the Son of God, who loved me and gave himself for me"* (Galatians 2:20). In other words, his secret weapon wasn't just his faith in God; it was God's faithfulness holding *him* steady.

Friend, be encouraged: You don't have to feel fearless. You don't have to have mountain-sized faith.

Even mustard-seed faith works when it's connected to an all-powerful God (Matthew 17:20).

Don't rehearse the problem. Don't magnify the giants. Don't keep speaking defeat over your life. Magnify God. Have a Joshua spirit. Be a Caleb. Speak healing when the report says otherwise. Speak abundance when things look tight. Speak victory when fear tries to take over. Your words aren't casual; they're creative and shaping the direction of your life!

When Caleb was eighty-five years old, decades after that first scouting trip to the Promised Land, he stood before Joshua and asked for the very hill country that once terrified the others. With strength in his voice, he said, *"Give me this mountain"* (Joshua 14:12, NKJV). The giants that once caused fear became the very proof of God's faithfulness. And he conquered them!

Fear-filled words lead to wilderness living. Faith-filled words lead to promised-land living. When fear tries to have the final word, gently but firmly answer back with faith — and speak like someone who knows the promise is already on the way. Because it is.

IF, RIGHT NOW, YOUR WORDS = FEAR . . .

“

~~*I'm outmatched.*~~

~~*I'll never get over this fear.*~~

~~*I'm afraid the future won't get any better.*~~

”

CHANGE THEM!
LET YOUR WORDS =
FAITH

"

The Lord fights for me.

With God, I am full of faith.

I will see God's goodness
in my lifetime.

"

SCRIPTURES FOR FAITH

Then Caleb silenced the people before Moses and said, "We should go up and take possession of the land, for we can certainly do it."

NUMBERS 13:30

"Only do not rebel against the LORD. And do not be afraid of the people of the land. . . . The LORD is with us. Do not be afraid of them."

NUMBERS 14:9

"Have I not commanded you? Be strong and courageous. Do not be afraid; do not be discouraged, for the LORD your God will be with you wherever you go."

JOSHUA 1:9

"I have been crucified with Christ and I no longer live, but Christ lives in me. The life I now live in the body, I live by faith in the Son of God, who loved me and gave himself for me."

GALATIANS 2:20

He replied, "Because you have so little faith. Truly I tell you, if you have faith as small as a mustard seed, you can say to this mountain, 'Move from here to there,' and it will move. Nothing will be impossible for you."

MATTHEW 17:20

The LORD is my light and my salvation—whom shall I fear? The LORD is the stronghold of my life—of whom shall I be afraid?

PSALM 27:1

"So do not fear, for I am with you; do not be dismayed, for I am your God."

ISAIAH 41:10

"When you pass through the waters, I will be with you."

ISAIAH 43:2

When I am afraid, I put my trust in you.

PSALM 56:3

Now faith is confidence in what we hope for and assurance about what we do not see.

HEBREWS 11:1

If God is for us, who can be against us?

ROMANS 8:31

"Don't be afraid; just believe."

MARK 5:36

There is no fear in love. But perfect love drives out fear.

1 JOHN 4:18

5

YOUR WORDS = PURPOSE OR PAIN

"You intended to harm me, but God intended it for good to accomplish what is now being done, the saving of many lives."

GENESIS 50:20

Joseph was just a teenager when life took a turn he never imagined.

God had given him big dreams of leadership, influence, and purpose — dreams where he saw himself helping people and making a difference. But the people closest to him didn't see those dreams as promises. They saw them as threats.

His brothers grew jealous. Every time Joseph shared what God showed him, it only stirred their resentment more. What could have been celebrated was criticized. What should have been encouraged was attacked. Finally, one day, their jealousy boiled over and they threw him into a pit.

Can you imagine the shock as Joseph looked up at the faces he trusted most, thinking, *Surely this is a mistake. Surely, they'll take me home?*

Instead, Joseph's brothers sold him into slavery. It looked like Joseph's story was over before it got a chance to begin.

In Egypt, he was sold again, this time into Potiphar's house. It would have been easy to get bitter and rehearse what his brothers had done.

But Joseph didn't let his heart go there. He kept honoring God. He kept doing the right thing when nobody was watching. And because of that, God's favor followed him. Before long, everything Joseph touched began to prosper. Potiphar trusted him with his whole household.

Then came another blow.

Potiphar's wife falsely accused Joseph, and he was thrown into prison for a crime he didn't commit. Another pit, and again, it didn't make sense. Again, it looked like life was going backward. But even there, in that dark cell, Joseph stayed faithful. He encouraged others. He interpreted dreams. He kept a good attitude when he had every reason to complain. And at just the right time, God opened a door no man could shut.

Pharaoh had a troubling dream, and he was desperate for someone to interpret it. Suddenly, Joseph's name came up. He was delivered out of the prison, cleaned up, and brought before the most powerful man in Egypt. After he interpreted Pharaoh's dream, he was promoted to second-in-command over the entire nation.

From the pit to the palace . . . only God can write a story like that.

Years passed, and a famine spread across the land. People from everywhere came to Egypt looking for food. One day, a group of tired, hungry men walked into the palace asking for help. Joseph looked up and his heart nearly stopped. It was his brothers!

They didn't recognize him. How could they? The frightened brother they sold into slavery was now dressed in royal robes, speaking with authority, a leader. But Joseph recognized them instantly.

All the memories came rushing back: the betrayal, the pit, the loneliness. He could have punished them. He had the power now; one word and their lives could have been over. But somewhere along the journey, God healed his heart.

Instead of revenge, Joseph felt compassion. When he finally revealed who he was, the room went silent. His brothers trembled, expecting judgment. But Joseph cried with tears of mercy. He said, *"Do not be afraid. . . . But as for you, you meant evil against me; but God meant it for good"* (Genesis 50:19–20, NKJV).

Think about that. Joseph didn't deny the pain. He simply refused to let pain define his purpose. Joseph could have spent his life talking about what his brothers did to him. Instead, he focused on what God did *for* him. And that made all the difference.

PURPOSE

PURPOSE DOESN'T MEAN PRETENDING EVERYTHING IS PERFECT. IT'S HAVING THE FAITH TO DECLARE, "GOD, I DON'T UNDERSTAND THIS, BUT MY LIFE IS IN YOUR HANDS. YOU SEE WHAT I CAN'T SEE. YOU ARE ORDERING MY STEPS. WHEN IT FEELS LIKE I'M WALKING IN CIRCLES, YOU ARE PREPARING THE WAY TO MY PURPOSE!"

As humans, we love clarity. We want a reason for every delay, disappointment, and closed door. Most of the time, however, God doesn't give us explanations. Instead, He invites us to trust Him.

When you look at Joseph's life from a distance, it reads like a beautiful story of promotion and favor. From the pit to the palace. From prisoner to prince. From forgotten to second-in-command over an entire nation. Yet, when you zoom in on the individual moments, the story doesn't look beautiful at all.

It looks confusing. It looks unfair. It looks painful. But life isn't one clean, finished picture. Oftentimes, it's more like a puzzle.

When you pick up one single piece by itself, it doesn't make sense. It may look dark, jagged, or completely out of place. You can't see how or where it belongs. But when the Master Builder starts putting all the pieces together, suddenly you realize that piece wasn't random at all. It was necessary.

Joseph could have stared at the broken pieces of his life. He could have replayed the betrayal, the false accusations, the lonely nights in prison, the years that felt stolen. And no one would have blamed him. Anyone else probably would have said, "God, this isn't fair. *You* are not fair. Why is this happening to me? How can I trust You?"

But Joseph made a decision that changed everything. He didn't ignore the pain, but he also didn't give it a voice. There's a difference.

We can often label ourselves by what's happened in our past. We relive disappointments with our words. Until, before long, we're not just walking through a hard season . . . we're living in it permanently.

But here's the good news I want to encourage you with today: The enemy didn't hijack your destiny. God didn't lose control. Your future wasn't derailed. You are still on schedule!

One of my favorite moments in Joseph's story comes after all the hardship and even the promotion. God blesses him with a son, and Joseph names him Manasseh, which means, "God has made me forget all my trouble."

I love that! Joseph did that not because the pain magically disappeared or the memories were erased but because the blessing became greater than the hurt. Joseph didn't get stuck in what wounded him. He lived grateful for the God who healed him. And that's God's heart for you too.

That closed door still might not make sense. That unfair criticism might still sting. That relationship that ended might still hurt. But God doesn't waste anything. He knows how to take what looks like a loss and use it as positioning for your purpose.

There is a Manasseh season coming—a season where God restores you so deeply, favors you so strongly, and blesses you so fully that what once felt overwhelming won't define you anymore.

Here's the key to remember: your words can determine how quickly you get there. You can speak pain, "This ruined my life. I'll never recover. It's too late for me." Or you can speak purpose, "God is still working. This is not the end. He's turning this for my good."

Your words don't change the past, but they absolutely shape the future.

Joseph chose purpose over pain, trust over understanding, faith over frustration. And when you do the same, you'll discover something powerful: what felt like the worst chapter of your life may actually be the very thing God uses to carry you into your greatest calling. So, keep trusting and believing, and keep speaking purpose.

I love what the Psalmist declares, *We went through fire and water, but you brought us to a place of abundance* (Psalm 66:12).

No doubt God is still putting pieces together in your life, and when He's finished, it's going to be more beautiful than you ever imagined. He knows how to turn every pit into preparation, every prison into promotion, and every painful chapter you've endured into purpose!

IF, RIGHT NOW, YOUR WORDS = **PAIN . . .**

"

~~*I'll always feel stuck.*~~

~~*I missed my chance.*~~

~~*My past defines me.*~~

"

CHANGE THEM!
LET YOUR WORDS =
PURPOSE

"

God is leading me forward into purpose.

God's timing is perfect.

God is redeeming my story and restoring my future!

"

SCRIPTURES FOR PURPOSE

"You intended to harm me, but God intended it for good to accomplish what is now being done, the saving of many lives."

GENESIS 50:20

"For I know the plans I have for you," declares the LORD, *"plans to prosper you and not to harm you, plans to give you hope and a future."*

JEREMIAH 29:11

And we know that in all things God works for the good of those who love him, who have been called according to his purpose.

ROMANS 8:28

The LORD *makes firm the steps of the one who delights in him; though he may stumble, he will not fall, for the* LORD *upholds him with his hand.*

PSALM 37:23–24

"For my thoughts are not your thoughts, neither are your ways my ways," declares the LORD. "As the heavens are higher than the earth, so are my ways higher than your ways and my thoughts than your thoughts."

ISAIAH 55:8–9

The LORD will vindicate me; your love, LORD, endures forever—do not abandon the works of your hands.

PSALM 138:8

In their hearts humans plan their course, but the LORD establishes their steps.

PROVERBS 16:9

Therefore we do not lose heart. Though outwardly we are wasting away, yet inwardly we are being renewed day by day. For our light and momentary troubles are achieving for us an eternal glory that far outweighs them all.

2 CORINTHIANS 4:16–17

For you, God, tested us; you refined us like silver. You brought us into prison and laid burdens on our backs . . . we went through fire and water, but you brought us to a place of abundance.

PSALM 66:10–12

I will instruct you and teach you in the way you should go; I will counsel you with my loving eye on you.

PSALM 32:8

The LORD is good to those whose hope is in him, to the one who seeks him; it is good to wait quietly for the salvation of the LORD.

LAMENTATIONS 3:25–26

You will keep in perfect peace those whose minds are steadfast, because they trust in you. Trust in the LORD forever, for the LORD, the LORD himself, is the Rock eternal.

ISAIAH 26:3–4

And the God of all grace, who called you to his eternal glory in Christ, after you have suffered a little while, will himself restore you and make you strong, firm and steadfast.

1 PETER 5:10

6

YOUR WORDS =

BREAKTHROUGH OR BONDAGE

About midnight Paul and Silas were praying and singing hymns to God, and the other prisoners were listening to them. Suddenly there was such a violent earthquake that the foundations of the prison were shaken. At once all the prison doors flew open, and everyone's chains came loose.

ACTS 16:25-26

Paul and Silas weren't in trouble because they had done something wrong.

They hadn't been reckless or dishonest. They weren't causing chaos or trying to stir up drama. In fact, their actions were the opposite. They were helping people, praying for the hurting, setting captives free, and bringing hope to a city that desperately needed it.

They were right in the center of God's will, doing exactly what they had been called to do. Yet somehow, doing the right thing landed them in the wrong place.

False accusations spread like wildfire. A small complaint turned into a crowd, and the crowd quickly became a mob. Before they even had a chance to explain themselves, they were beaten with rods and publicly humiliated. It was swift and unfair, the kind of situation that makes you shake your head and think, *God, how could You let this happen?*

Then it got worse.

They weren't placed in a comfortable holding cell or somewhere near the light. They were thrown into the innermost prison — the dungeon — the darkest, coldest, most suffocating part of the jail.

If anyone had a reason to complain, it was them.

But Paul and Silas weren't normal. Around midnight, when the adrenaline had worn off, when the pain had settled deep into their bones, when exhaustion and discouragement usually grow the loudest, they made a decision that changed everything.

Instead of replaying the injustice, instead of blaming God, they began to pray. And not long after that, they started to sing. It wasn't soft humming under their breath or a whispered song to themselves. Scripture says they praised God loud enough that the other prisoners could hear them.

Picture it for a moment. Two men, bruised and chained in the dark, lifting their voices in worship.

I can imagine the other inmates looking at them and thinking, *What is wrong with these guys? Don't they realize where they are? Don't they see how bad that looks?* But Paul and Silas understood something: Praise isn't based on circumstances. Praise is based on who God is.

They knew that, even in a dungeon, God was still God. Even when they were in chains, He was still faithful. Even when life didn't make sense, He was still working behind the scenes.

Suddenly, without warning, the ground began to shake. An earthquake ripped through that prison so violently the foundations trembled. Doors flew open. Chains fell off. The very stocks that had held them tight loosened their grip.

In one moment, what had bound them couldn't hold them anymore. They didn't force the doors open. They didn't fight their way out. They didn't argue their case. Their praise made room for God to move.

Breakthrough didn't come while they were complaining — it came while they were worshiping.

If they had spent the night bitter and grumbling, they probably would have stayed prisoners. But their words shifted the atmosphere. Their attitude invited God's power. An uncommon response brought an uncommon breakthrough. And what once looked like bondage became the very place God displayed His freedom.

BREAKTHROUGH

SOMETIMES ONE SONG IN THE NIGHT, ONE WHISPERED PRAYER, OR ONE DECLARATION OF PRAISE IS ALL IT TAKES FOR GOD TO SHAKE THE FOUNDATIONS OF WHAT'S BEEN HOLDING YOU BACK AND BRING BREAKTHROUGH. AND THE SAME GOD WHO FREED PAUL AND SILAS IS STILL FREEING PEOPLE TODAY!

Creation began in darkness. Seeds grow quietly underground long before they ever break the surface. Even the new day technically starts at midnight, when the sun is nowhere to be seen.

God has a pattern of starting new things in places that don't look promising. But when you begin to understand that, it can change the way you view difficult seasons. You won't panic as quickly. You won't assume darkness means defeat. Instead, you'll realize that sometimes the very thing that feels like an ending is the moment God begins working behind the scenes.

Think about Paul and Silas sitting there in that inner cell, chains around their feet, their backs bruised and aching, guards at the doors. Every circumstance said, "This is final." Every voice of reason would have told them to be discouraged. But people don't have the final say — God does.

What you're up against may look bigger and stronger, but you and God are a majority. If He is for you, it doesn't matter who is against you. There isn't an obstacle He can't move, a sickness He can't heal, or an addiction He can't break.

Paul and Silas could have spent that night complaining. They could have replayed everything that went wrong. "God, this isn't fair. We were doing what You asked." But instead, at midnight, when the pain was sharpest and the darkness deepest, they began to pray and praise.

Some of my favorite moments at church haven't come while I'm on the platform speaking. They've happened while I'm standing with the congregation singing, worshiping and praising God with Victoria.

We don't praise God out of obligation. We praise Him because He is worthy of it. And I've seen firsthand — week after week, year after year — how worship changes our circumstances, our hearts, and our perspective.

By the grace of God, our children are now part of leading worship each weekend. It makes me smile because not only is it a joy seeing my kids bring glory to God; they've also recognized the immense power of praising Him.

Have you? Do you know how worshiping God impacts situations and lives far beyond what you might comprehend?

In 2 Kings 6, we find Elisha and his servant surrounded by a powerful army. The servant panicked, thinking they were outnumbered. But Elisha prayed, *"Open his eyes, Lord"* (v. 17). Suddenly, the servant saw the hills around them full of horses and chariots of fire.

They weren't surrounded by the enemy. The enemy was surrounded by the angel armies of Almighty God!

Likewise, when you feel surrounded, praise opens your spiritual eyes to God's presence so you know His power is greater than whatever's against you.

I don't know what battle you're facing right now — whether it's in your health, your finances, your family, or your future — but I want to encourage you: You're not outnumbered. The enemy is! While you're worshiping, God is working.

For Paul and Silas, they may have been praising at ten o'clock and nothing happened. Perhaps they were thanking God at eleven, still, no change. Maybe they were singing at eleven thirty and everything looked the same. But when midnight came, suddenly, everything shifted.

The ground shook. The doors flew open. The chains fell off. The miracle didn't start after they got free. It started while they worshiped.

Today, don't let your words lock you in a prison of your own making. Choose praise over complaint, faith over fear, and breakthrough over bondage.

Anybody can complain and get bitter. Anybody can rehearse what went wrong. But when you choose to worship God anyway, that's what releases breakthrough in the atmosphere! And your freedom is only the beginning. Look at what happened next in the story:

> *The jailer woke up, and when he saw the prison doors open, he drew his sword and was about to kill himself because he thought the prisoners had escaped. But Paul shouted, "Don't harm yourself! We are all here!"*
>
> *The jailer called for lights, rushed in and fell trembling before Paul and Silas. He then brought them out and asked, "Sirs, what must I do to be saved?"*

> *They replied, "Believe in the Lord Jesus, and you will be saved—you and your household." Then they spoke the word of the Lord to him and to all the others in his house. . . . He was filled with joy because he had come to believe in God—he and his whole household.*
> Acts 16:27–34

There are people around you who need the same hope you have in Jesus. So, as God frees you, be attentive to the people in your life who notice, who are curious, who need their own breakthrough.

There's no limit to what God can do in you. And there's also no limit to what He wants to do *through* you!

IF, RIGHT NOW, YOUR WORDS = BONDAGE . . .

"

~~*I will never break free from this.*~~

~~*Nothing is ever going to change.*~~

~~*I feel trapped and stuck.*~~

"

CHANGE THEM! LET YOUR WORDS = BREAKTHROUGH

"*He whom the Son sets free is free indeed!*

Even now, I praise God for doing a new thing!

God is delivering me from this darkness and breaking every chain!"

SCRIPTURES FOR BREAKTHROUGH

"The One who breaks open the way will go up before them; they will break through the gate and go out. Their King will pass through before them, the LORD at their head."

MICAH 2:13

LORD, you are my God; I will exalt you and praise your name, for in perfect faithfulness you have done wonderful things, things planned long ago.

ISAIAH 25:1

"See, I am doing a new thing! Now it springs up; do you not perceive it? I am making a way in the wilderness and streams in the wasteland."

ISAIAH 43:19

The righteous person may have many troubles, but the LORD delivers him from them all.

PSALM 34:19

Not one of all the LORD's good promises to Israel failed; every one was fulfilled.

JOSHUA 21:45

Through you we push back our enemies; through your name we trample our foes.

PSALM 44:5

He brought them out of darkness, the utter darkness, and broke away their chains.

PSALM 107:14

Now to him who is able to do immeasurably more than all we ask or imagine, according to his power that is at work within us.

EPHESIANS 3:20

"So if the Son sets you free, you will be free indeed."

JOHN 8:36

It is for freedom that Christ has set us free. Stand firm, then, and do not let yourselves be burdened again by a yoke of slavery.

GALATIANS 5:1

But the Lord is faithful, and he will strengthen you and protect you from the evil one.

2 THESSALONIANS 3:3

You armed me with strength for battle;
you humbled my adversaries before me.

PSALM 18:39

Submit yourselves, then, to God. Resist the devil, and he will flee from you.

JAMES 4:7

For we know that our old self was crucified with him so that the body ruled by sin might be done away with, that we should no longer be slaves to sin—because anyone who has died has been set free from sin.

ROMANS 6:6–7

"The Spirit of the Lord is on me, because he has anointed me to proclaim good news to the poor. He has sent me to proclaim freedom for the prisoners and recovery of sight for the blind, to set the oppressed free, to proclaim the year of the Lord's favor."

LUKE 4:18–19

7

YOUR WORDS = COURAGE OR COMPROMISE

"Yet who knows whether you have come to the kingdom for such a time as this?"

ESTHER 4:14 (NKJV)

Esther wasn't born into royalty or influence. She didn't grow up with connections or privilege. She was an orphan, raised by her older cousin Mordecai.

At the time, Israel had been conquered by Babylon and many Jews remained in exile in the country. But when the king began searching the empire for a new queen, Esther was swept into a world she never would have chosen for herself.

One day she was at home; the next she was in the palace, surrounded by luxury, protocol, and pressure. There, God gave her favor. Out of all the women brought before the king, he chose Esther to become queen.

From the outside, it looked like fortune. From Heaven's perspective, it was positioning.

While Esther was learning palace life, something dark was unfolding behind the scenes. A powerful official named Haman, fueled by hatred and pride, convinced the king to sign a decree ordering the destruction of the Jewish people throughout the empire.

When Mordecai heard the news, grief overwhelmed him. He put on sackcloth and ashes and wept openly in the streets. Eventually, word reached Esther. The people marked for death weren't strangers. They were her family, her heritage, her story. Esther was a Jew, but on Mordecai's advice, she had kept this hidden. The king didn't know he had declared the death of his very queen.

Esther faced a crossroads. She needed to speak to the king but doing so uninvited could lead to her death. One misstep and she would be executed on the spot. To make matters worse, the previous queen had been deposed for disrespecting the king. Esther had good reason to hesitate. Maybe she hoped someone else would step forward. But Mordecai sent her a message that wouldn't let her hide:

> *"Do not think that because you are in the king's house you alone of all the Jews will escape. For if you remain silent at this time, relief and deliverance for the Jews will arise from another place, but you and your father's family will perish. And who knows but that you have come to your royal position for such a time as this?"*
> Esther 4:13–14

In that moment, Esther realized the crown wasn't for comfort. It was for responsibility. She responded:

> *"Go, gather together all the Jews who are in Susa, and fast for me. Do not eat or drink for three days, night or day. I and my attendants will fast as you do. When this is done, I will go to the king, even though it is against the law. And if I perish, I perish."* Esther 4:16

There must have been a holy stillness in her heart as she walked toward the throne room. When the king saw her, the seconds must have felt endless. Slowly, he extended the gold scepter — the simple gesture that meant life instead of death.

With wisdom and patience, Esther invited him to a banquet, then another, waiting for the right moment to speak.

When she finally shared the truth, exposing Haman's plan and identifying herself with her people, her voice carried both courage and conviction. The king's anger rose against Haman, the plot unraveled, and the very decree meant to destroy the Jews was reversed.

An entire nation lived because one woman refused to remain quiet.

Esther could have compromised and preserved her comfort. Instead, she chose courage, and God moved in ways she never could have arranged herself!

COURAGE

GOD ISN'T LOOKING FOR PERFECTION OR IMPRESSIVE RÉSUMÉS. HE'S SEARCHING FOR SOMEONE WITH THE COURAGE TO SAY, "HERE I AM, LORD. USE ME."

Esther wasn't the most connected person. She didn't come from influence or wealth or have a family name that opened doors. She didn't grow up training for a throne or imagining that history would remember her story.

By every outward measure, Esther was ordinary. But she possessed something far more powerful than credentials — the courage to be *willing*.

Courage doesn't always look loud or dramatic. Sometimes it's simply the decision to trust God enough to take the next step when your hands are shaking.

It's choosing obedience when staying comfortable would be easier. It's moving forward even when you don't have all the answers.

Each of us is given moments — opportunities placed in our path — where we sense that what we choose matters. What we do with those invitations shapes our story. And Esther's life is a beautiful picture of this.

Through a series of unlikely events only God could orchestrate, she found herself in the palace, wearing a crown she never imagined she would wear.

For a while, life may have felt settled. The palace walls offered protection. Her position offered security. She could have kept enjoying the favor surrounding her and never stepped beyond it.

Then came the news that changed everything.

Her people were threatened with destruction. An entire nation faced annihilation. Suddenly, Esther realized that the place she stood — the very position she hadn't planned or pursued — gave her access no one else had.

Approaching the king uninvited wasn't a small thing; it could cost her life. So, you can imagine the internal battle that may have happened within her. The questions. The fear.

What if the king refuses to see me? What if I lose everything? What if stepping out costs too much?

Compromise often magnifies risk. It offers the easier option to stay silent and safe.

This is why we all need a "Mordecai" in our lives, someone to remind and exhort us not to sit on the sidelines but step out with boldness when the moment calls for it.

For Esther, Mordecai gently reminded her that perhaps her life had positioned her for this very opportunity — not by accident or chance but by divine design. Not because she was forced into something, but because she was invited to be part of something bigger than herself.

So, Esther did something brave. She didn't rush ahead in panic. She prayed. She fasted. She gathered others to pray with her. Esther anchored her heart in God before she ever stepped into that throne room.

Then, with no guarantees and no control over the outcome, she walked forward. And when the king extended his scepter, favor met her courage.

What looked like an impossible situation shifted because one woman chose courage over compromise. And that same invitation rests before you today.

You may never stand in a palace or plead for a nation, but rest assured, you will face moments that ask for courage — moments when speaking up, stepping out, forgiving, serving, or trusting feels risky. Moments where you could stay comfortable and choose to be safe.

Those are your Esther moments. Those are your *opportunities* to partner with God, to see what He can do with a willing heart.

The prophet Joel said, "*Wake up the mighty men*" (Joel 3:9, NKJV). In other words, don't sleep through your calling. Don't live distracted. Don't let fear or comfort keep you hidden.

Jesus also said in Matthew 5:14–16, "*You are the light of the world. A town built on a hill cannot be hidden. Neither do people light a lamp and put it under a bowl. Instead they put it on its stand, and it gives light to everyone in the house. In the same way, let your light shine before others, that they may see your good deeds and glorify your Father in heaven.*"

Make no mistake: You are not average. You are not reading this by accident. You are a history-maker and a world-changer. God wants you to leave your mark on this generation. But there's an enemy who knows that too. And one of his most effective tools is procrastination.

If he can't convince you to quit, he'll try to convince you to wait.

"Tomorrow."
"Later."
"When it's easier."
"When you feel more qualified."

Procrastination sounds harmless. It sounds reasonable. But "later" has perhaps stolen more destinies than failure ever has.

Scripture says, *"Today, if you hear his voice, do not harden your hearts"* (Hebrews 3:15). Today. Not someday. Not eventually. Today!

Don't talk yourself out of what God has placed in front of you. Don't assume someone else will do it better. Choose courage. *Speak* courage. Because you may discover that the very places where you once felt small or unqualified are the exact places God can work through you most powerfully.

Like Esther, you'll look back and realize you were placed there by God so your courage could rise, your faith could move, and God could work through you in ways you never imagined possible.

IF, RIGHT NOW, YOUR WORDS = COMPROMISE . . .

"

~~It's safer if I stay quiet.~~

~~I don't want to stand out.~~

~~Someone else will handle it.~~

"

CHANGE THEM! LET YOUR WORDS = COURAGE

"

God has not given me a spirit of fear but of power, love, and a sound mind.

I was created to shine, not shrink back.

God chose me for this moment, and I will step up!

"

SCRIPTURES FOR COURAGE

Wait for the Lord; be strong and take
heart and wait for the Lord.

PSALM 27:14

For the Spirit God gave us does not make us
timid, but gives us power, love and self-discipline.

2 TIMOTHY 1:7

Be strong, and let your heart take courage,
all you who wait for the Lord!

PSALM 31:24 (ESV)

Even though I walk through the darkest valley,
I will fear no evil, for you are with me.

PSALM 23:4

The wicked flee though no one pursues,
but the righteous are as bold as a lion.

PROVERBS 28:1

"Do not fear, for I have redeemed you; I have summoned you by name; you are mine."

ISAIAH 43:1

So we say with confidence, "The Lord is my helper; I will not be afraid. What can mere mortals do to me?"

HEBREWS 13:6

Pray also for me, that whenever I speak, words may be given me so that I will fearlessly make known the mystery of the gospel.

EPHESIANS 6:19

Be on your guard; stand firm in the faith; be courageous; be strong.

1 CORINTHIANS 16:13

This is the confidence we have in approaching God: that if we ask anything according to his will, he hears us.

1 JOHN 5:14

"Peace I leave with you; my peace I give to you.Not as the world gives do I give to you. Let not your hearts be troubled, neither let them be afraid."

JOHN 14:27 (ESV)

They will have no fear of bad news; their hearts are steadfast, trusting in the LORD.

PSALM 112:7

Finally, be strong in the Lord and in his mighty power.

EPHESIANS 6:10

So do not throw away your confidence; it will be richly rewarded. You need to persevere so that when you have done the will of God, you will receive what he has promised.

HEBREWS 10:35–36

ABOUT JOEL OSTEEN MINISTRIES

Joel Osteen Ministries, rooted in Houston, Texas, is an extension of the legacy built by John and Dodie Osteen, who founded Lakewood Church in 1959. Originally meeting in a modest feed store, Lakewood has grown into one of the largest congregations in the U.S., attracting people from all walks of life. John Osteen's leadership touched millions through his television ministry, which reached over 100 countries, and his influence as a pastor's pastor. His wife, Dodie, also played a key role, especially with her testimony of miraculous healing from cancer, which has inspired countless people.

When John passed away in 1999, his son Joel stepped into leadership, despite his background in television production. Joel's transition into senior pastor marked a new era for Lakewood, with the church's global influence expanding significantly. Under Joel's leadership, Lakewood's outreach grew, broadcasting to over 200 million households, and the church became a beacon of hope for millions seeking encouragement and inspiration.

Joel's wife, Victoria, serves alongside him, contributing to the church's leadership and vision. Their daughter, Alexandra, continues the family tradition, leading worship and contributing to Lakewood Music. With a focus on uplifting messages and practical teachings, Joel Osteen Ministries aims to reach new generations, inspiring people worldwide to rise above their challenges and live their best life through faith, hope, and love.